Vegetables and Salads

Library of Congress Cataloging-in-Publication Data

De Villiers, Stoffelina Johanna Adriana.
Vegetables and salads.

(First cookbook library / S.J.A. de Villiers and
E. van der Berg)
Includes index.
Summary: Introduces young chefs to the preparation
of vegetables and salads.
1. Cookery (Vegetables)—Juvenile literature.
2. Salads—Juvenile literature. [1. Cookery—
Vegetables. 2. Salads] I. Van der Berg, Eunice.
II. Johnson, Marita, ill. III. Title. IV. Series:
De Villiers, Stoffelina Johanna Adriana.
First cookbook library.

TX801.D4 1985 641.6'5 85-12698
ISBN 0-918831-78-4
ISBN 0-918831-33-4 (lib. bdg.)

ISBN 0-918831-33-4 lib. bdg.
ISBN 0-918831-78-4 trade bdg.

Series Editor: MaryLee Knowlton
Cover Illustrations: Renée Graef
Typeset by Superior Printing • Milwaukee, Wisconsin 53223, USA

Vegetables and Salads

S.J.A. de Villiers
and
Eunice van der Berg

Illustrated By
Marita Johnson

Gareth Stevens Publishing
Milwaukee

First Cookbook Library

Getting Ready To Cook
Drinks and Desserts
One Dish Meals
Vegetables and Salads
Breads and Biscuits
Cookies, Cakes, and Candies

These books will show you how easy it is to cook and what fun it is, too.

Everything you have to do is clearly illustrated and the methods you will learn are the same as those used in advanced cookbooks. Once you learn these methods, you will be able to follow recipes you find in any cookbook.

This book will show you how to prepare and cook vegetables. It will teach you how to make and serve salads. Any one of these recipes will make a healthy addition to every meal.

If you are concerned about salt, sugar, and fats in your diet, you may reduce the amount called for or substitute other ingredients in many of the recipes. Ask a grown-up for suggestions.

More information about nutrition, ingredients, and cooking methods can be found in GETTING READY TO COOK, a companion volume to this book.

CONTENTS

Black arrows ➡ in some recipes are reminders to ask a grown-up to help you.

Crisp Salad
(4 to 6 servings)

(check pages 30 and 31 for vegetable dip recipes)

Take Out:

cutting board
vegetable knife
vegetable peeler
measuring spoons
large mixing bowl
wooden tray or server

Besides the fruits and vegetables listed below, you can add others that you would like to serve with them.

What You'll Need

6 small carrots
4 to 6 crisp lettuce leaves
2 tomatoes
1 cucumber
2 celery stalks
1 pineapple
1 green pepper
1 head of cauliflower
1 teaspoon salt

How to Prepare Salad Ingredients:

1. Wash carrots, green peppers, celery, tomatoes,

and cucumbers in cold water in the sink.

2. Empty the sink and rinse the vegetables under cold running water. Do not bruise the vegetables.

3. Dissolve the salt in a quart of cold water in the mixing bowl.

4. Wash the lettuce leaves, one at a time, in the salt water.

➡ 5. Cut the flowers off the cauliflower and wash each piece in the salt water.

6. Pour out the salt water and rinse the bowl with fresh water. Pour ice water into the mixing bowl and immerse the lettuce leaves and cauliflower pieces for five minutes.

7. Drain the water off the lettuce leaves and cauliflower.

8. Arrange the vegetables in rows on the wooden tray.

How to Peel and Cut Salad Ingredients:

Carrots

➡ 1. Peel the carrots with a vegetable peeler using long strokes away from you.

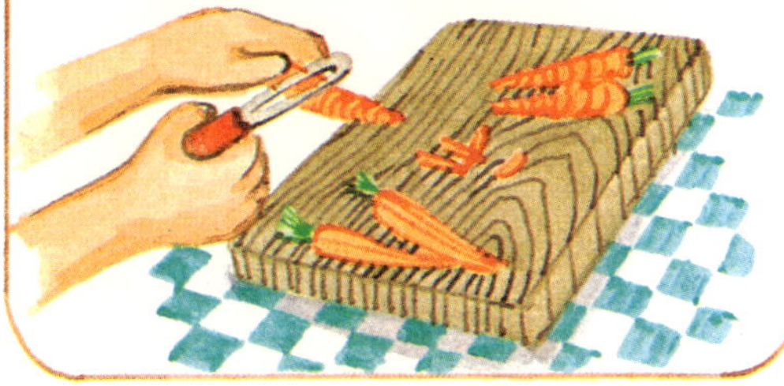

➡ 2. Cut off the thick ends with the vegetable knife.

3. Rinse once again and arrange on the tray.

Green Pepper

➡ 1. Cut the pepper into rings on the cutting board.

➡ 2. Cut away all the seeds and white ridges on the inside of each ring.

3. Arrange the rings in a row next to the other vegetables on the wooden tray.

Pineapple

➡ 1. Cut away one inch of each end of the pineapple using the vegetable knife on the cutting board.

➡ 2. Stand the pineapple on one end and peel in long thin strips from top to bottom.

➡ 3. Cut out the eyes with the tip of the vegetable knife.

4. Discard the peels and wash the board to remove all thorny bits.

➡ 5. Now cut the pineapple into round slices and arrange them in a row on the tray.

Celery Stalks

➡ 1. Cut away the leaves and white ends.

➡ 2. Cut each stalk into two-inch sticks and arrange them on the tray.

Tomatoes

➡ 1. Cut the tomatoes into two halves from top to bottom. Remove the white stem ends.

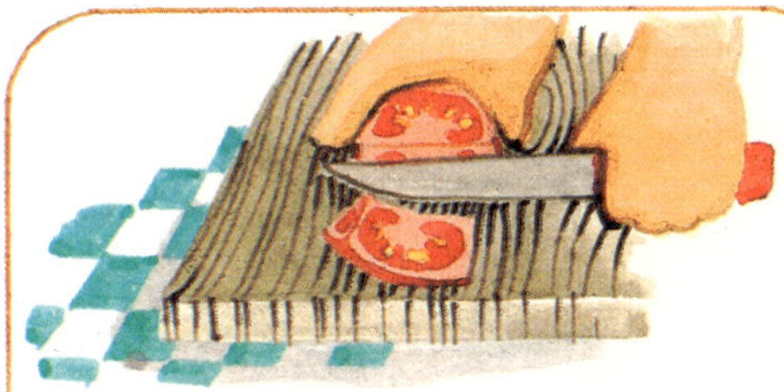

➡ 2. Cut each half into three wedges and arrange them in a row on the tray.

Cucumbers

➡ 1. Cut about one inch off the cucumber to remove the stem ends.

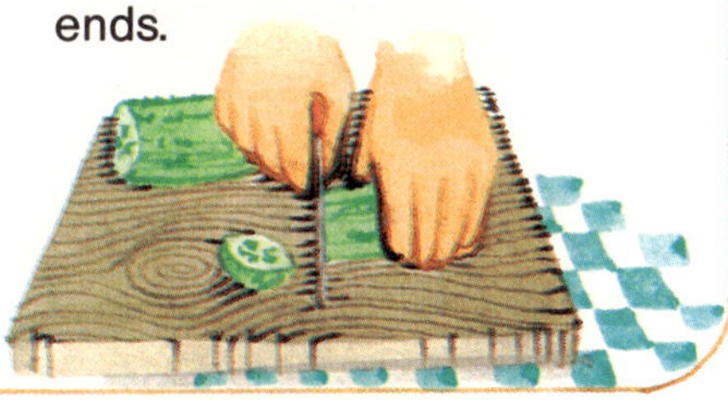

➡ 2. Peel it with a vegetable peeler, working away from yourself.

➡ 3. Cut the cucumber into thin slices and arrange them in a row on the tray next to the other vegetables.

Tossed Green Salad
(4 servings)

Take Out:

salad bowl
vegetable peeler
cutting board
vegetable knife
measuring cups
measuring spoons
mixing bowl
salad servers

What You'll Need

12 crisp lettuce leaves
½ small cucumber
2 tomatoes
4 green onions
pinch of salt
avocado
¼ cup salad dressing

1. Wash and dry the lettuce leaves and break them into small pieces in the salad bowl.

➡ 2. Peel the cucumber and cut it into cubes. Spread it over the lettuce.

➡ 3. Wash and cut the tomatoes into wedges. Arrange them over the cucumber.

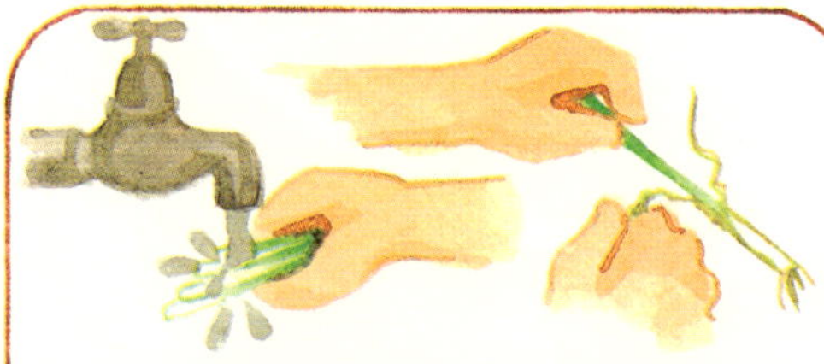

➡ 4. Wash the onions under cold running water. Pull off the thin outer skin and cut off the roots and some of the green leaves.

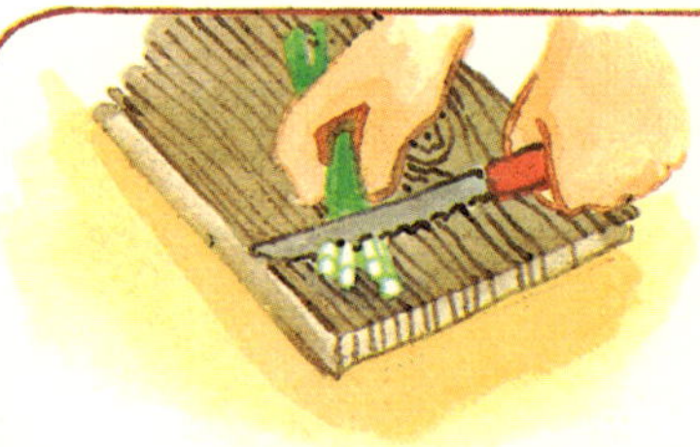

➡ 5. Cut the onions into small rings and sprinkle them over the tomato in the salad bowl.

➡ 6. Cut the avocado lengthwise into two halves and remove the pit. Peel each half carefully.

➡ 7. Dice the avocado and arrange it over the other layers. Ripe avocado bruises easily, so be careful!

8. Shake the bottle of dressing and pour ¼ cup over the salad just before serving.

9. Toss the salad and dressing lightly using the salad servers. Move the salad around until all the ingredients are evenly coated with the dressing.

Banana Salad
(4 servings)

Take Out:

orange juicer
shallow dish
mixing bowl
egg beater
vegetable knife
cutting board
knife, tablespoon
measuring cups
measuring spoons
salad bowl

What You'll Need

3 ripe bananas
1 lemon
1 cup mandarin oranges
¼ cup mayonnaise
½ cup whipping cream
2 teaspoons sugar
2 tablespoons chopped pecans

Note: Canned apricot halves may be used instead of oranges.

➡ 1. Cut the lemon in half on the cutting board. Use the orange juicer to squeeze out the juice. Pour the juice into the shallow dish.

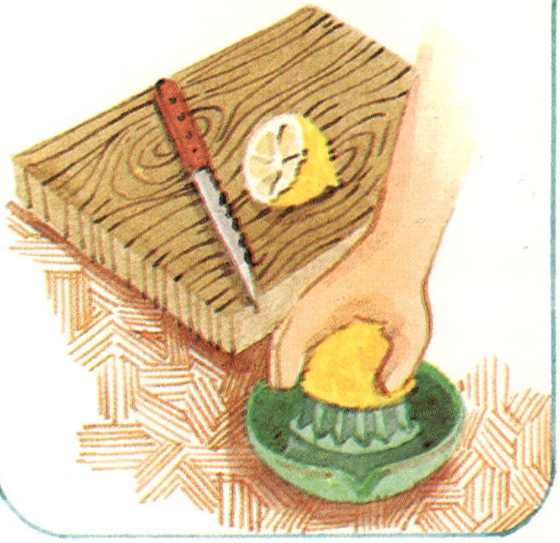

2. Peel the bananas and roll each one in the lemon juice to prevent them from browning.

➡ 3. Slice the bananas in rings and dice the orange slices on the cutting board.

4. Whip the cream in the mixing bowl until it becomes thick and clings to the blade of the egg beater. Do not beat longer than necessary.

5. Fold the sugar and mayonnaise into whipped cream using the tablespoon.

6. Spoon half the banana pieces and half the orange pieces into the salad bowl. Spread half the cream mixture over the fruit.

7. Repeat with a second layer of fruit and cover with the rest of the cream dressing. Sprinkle the chopped pecans over the top for decoration.

Boiled Potatoes

(4 servings)

Take Out:

saucepan
vegetable brush
vegetable knife
cutting board
measuring spoons
serving dish
tablespoon
potholders

What You'll Need

4 medium potatoes
½ teaspoon salt
butter

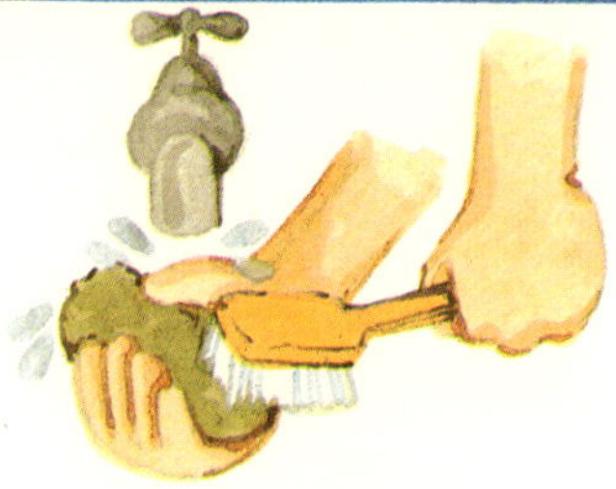

1. Scrub the potatoes with the vegetable brush under running water to remove all the dirt.

➡ 2. Cut each potato through lengthwise on the cutting board.

3. Put the potatoes in the saucepan with the skin-side down. Add two cups of hot water and put the lid on the saucepan.

➡ 4. Put the saucepan on a burner turned to high. When the water starts boiling, reduce the heat to medium.

➡ 5. Leave to cook until there is no water left. The potatoes should boil for at least 20 minutes. If they boil dry before 20 minutes are over, add a little water to the saucepan.

➡ 6. Sprinkle the salt over the potato halves in the saucepan. Use a tablespoon to place them on the serving dish.

7. Dot each potato half with butter before serving.

Baked Potatoes
(4 servings)

Take Out:

vegetable brush
vegetable knife
fork
oven mitts
clean dishcloth
serving plate

What You'll Need

4 medium potatoes
butter

➡ 1. Preheat the oven to 400°.

2. Scrub the potatoes with the vegetable brush under running water. Remove all the dirt.

3. Prick each potato three times with a fork to prevent its skin from bursting in the oven.

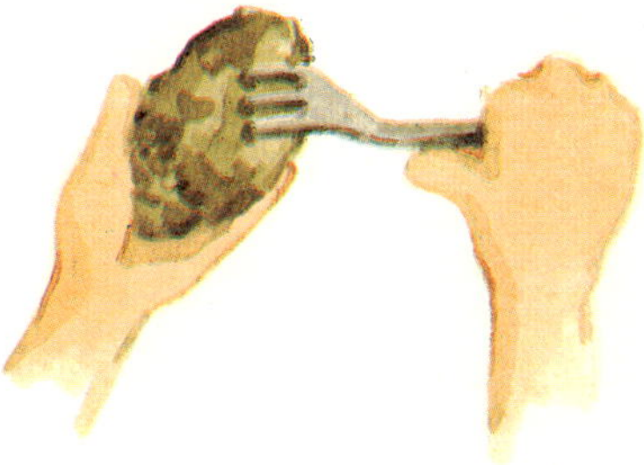

➡ 4. Place the potatoes on an oven rack in the middle of the oven. Leave to bake for one hour. Switch off the oven.

➡ 5. Take them from the oven using oven mitts. They will feel soft if they are ready. Place them on the serving plate.

6. Roll the potatoes, one at a time, in the dishcloth. This will loosen the skin.

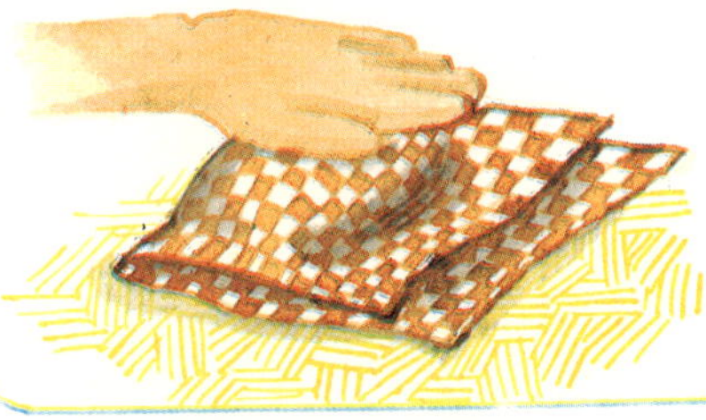

➡ 7. Cut a cross through the skin of each potato using the dishcloth to hold the potato. Squeeze each potato slightly to open at the cross until the white shows.

8. Serve with a pat of butter on the cross of each potato.

Boiled Carrots
(4 servings)

Take Out:

cutting board
vegetable knife
vegetable peeler
measuring cups
measuring spoons
saucepan
tablespoon
small serving bowl

What You'll Need

enough carrots to fill 2 cups when cut into rounds
pinch of salt
1 tablespoon butter
1 sprig of parsley

➡ 1. Wash and scrape the carrots (see page 9). Wash the parsley.

➡ 2. Slice the carrots thinly into rounds and put two cups of these into the saucepan.

➡ 3. Cover the carrots with hot water and put the lid on the saucepan.

➡ 4. Put the saucepan on the burner turned to high. As soon as the water boils, reduce the heat to medium.

➡ 5. Leave to boil for 15 minutes or until all the water has evaporated.

➡ 6. Turn off the heat and add the salt to the carrots. Spoon the carrots into the serving bowl.

7. Dot the carrots with butter and decorate with the sprig of parsley.

Boiled Green Beans

(4 to 6 servings)

Take Out:

cutting board
vegetable knife
saucepan
measuring cups
measuring spoons
fork
serving dish

What You'll Need

2 cups green beans
1 cup hot water
pinch of salt
1 tablespoon butter

Green peas, lima beans, young squashes, broccoli, cauliflower, and cabbage can be cooked in the same way.

1. Wash the beans in cold running water.

2. Cut off the stems. Slice the beans. Young green beans may be cooked whole.

3. Pour the water into the saucepan. Turn the burner to high and allow the water to boil.

4. Add the beans to the boiling water. Put the lid on the saucepan. Reduce the heat to medium.

5. Add the salt after 15 minutes. Prick the beans with a fork to test for tenderness.

6. Add a little extra water if the beans are still too firm and the water has boiled dry.

7. Leave to cook until all the water has evaporated. Turn off the heat.

8. Serve the beans in the serving dish and dot with pieces of butter.

Cooking Frozen Vegetables
(4 servings)

Take Out:

saucepan
measuring cups
measuring spoons
fork
serving dish

What You'll Need

1 package frozen vegetables
¼ cup water
pinch of salt
1 tablespoon butter

1. Measure the water into the saucepan. Add the salt.

➡ 2. Place the saucepan over a burner turned to high.

➡ 3. As soon as the water boils, add the frozen vegetables.

➡ 4. Reduce the heat to medium when it starts to boil again. Leave to cook for about four minutes.

➡ 5. Prick the vegetables with the fork to test for tenderness.

➡ 6. Remove the lid as soon as the vegetables are tender so that the remaining water can boil dry rapidly.

➡ 7. Watch all the time so that the vegetables do not burn when there is no water left. Turn off the heat.

8. Spoon the vegetables into a serving dish. Dot with pieces of butter.

Boiled Rice
(6 servings)

Take Out:

saucepan
measuring cups
measuring spoons
fork
wooden spoon
serving dish

What You'll Need

2 cups hot water
1 teaspoon salt
1 cup rice

Note: Cooking instructions may vary according to the brand of rice used. Check the package.

➡ 1. Pour the hot water into the saucepan. Turn on the burner to medium heat. Allow the water to boil.

➡ 2. Add the salt and rice. Stir with a wooden spoon. Leave to boil and do not stir any longer.

➡ 3. Reduce the heat to low. Cover the saucepan and leave it to simmer for 20 minutes.

➡ 4. The rice grains will be swollen and there should be no water left at the bottom. Small holes will have formed in the rice. Turn off the heat.

5. Loosen the rice with the fork and spoon it into the serving dish.

Cream of Vegetable Soup
(6 servings)

Take Out:

1 large saucepan
scissors
wooden spoon
can opener
measuring cups
6 soup bowls
6 soup spoons
1 soup ladle

What You'll Need

1 package beef soup mix
2 cups cold water
2 cups hot water
1 can cream of vegetable soup
1 cup milk
3 sprigs of parsley

1. Cut open the package of soup and empty it into the saucepan. Add the cold water and stir, using the wooden spoon, until smooth. Add the warm water.

➡ 2. Place the saucepan on a burner and turn on the heat to medium. Stir until the soup starts boiling.

➡ 3. Put the lid on at an angle to prevent the soup from boiling over. Reduce the heat to low. Leave to simmer for five minutes.

➡ 4. Use the can opener to open the vegetable soup. Stir the contents into the hot soup. Stir until it boils again. Add the milk and stir. Heat but do not boil.

➡ 5. Shred the parsley into the soup using the kitchen scissors.

6. Serve with bread and butter for lunch or supper.

Vegetable Dips

Use any one of these recipes to make a dip for the crisp salad (page 6).

Horseradish Dip

Blend these ingredients in a mixing bowl:

1 cup sour cream
1 tablespoon horseradish
¼ teaspoon salt
¼ teaspoon paprika

Oriental Ginger Dip

Blend these ingredients in a mixing bowl:

1 cup sour cream
2 tablespoons chopped ginger
1 tablespoon soy sauce
3 tablespoons mayonnaise
½ cup chopped green onions
3 tablespoons chopped water chestnuts

Dill Dip

Blend these ingredients in a mixing bowl:

1 cup sour cream
2 tablespoons dillweed
1 teaspoon onion salt
1 teaspoon celery salt
1 teaspoon sugar

Cream Cheese Dip

6 ounces cream cheese
2 tablespoons mayonnaise
1 tablespoon sour cream
pinch of salt
2 teaspoons fresh chives
1 teaspoon Worcestershire sauce

INDEX

Black arrows ➡ in some recipes are reminders to ask a grown-up to help you.